Invite a Bird

to Dinner

Simple Feeders You Can Make

BEVERLY COURTNEY CROOK
illustrated by Tom Huffman

Lothrop, Lee & Shepard Company
A Division of William Morrow & Company, Inc.
New York

For Beth, Keith,
Donna, Ronnie,
and Timothy Stephen

I wish to thank Compton N. Crook,
biology professor, bird bander,
and perennial bird student, for his
advice and encouragement.

Contents

0/27/79

Introduction

Invite a bird to dinner? Do you mean setting an extra place at the table for a blue jay or a woodpecker?

Yes. Not at your table, of course, but at a bird feeder that you have made.

But I don't know anything about bird feeders.

Then this is the book for you. Here are directions for making many different kinds of feeders as well as a "menu" to help you select food for a bird dinner—or breakfast or lunch. The feeders are easy to make and cost very little or nothing at all. Most of them are made from things found around the house—things that you often throw away.

Why should I feed the birds? They seem to be getting along all right without any help from me.

Birds manage to find their own food most of the year, that's true. But in cold weather, especially when snow or ice covers the ground, they have a hard time getting enough to eat. Then many birds die without help from their human friends. Your feeders could make the difference between life and death for them.

Besides, birds are great fun to watch! You'll agree when they discover your "table." Some will come shyly, grab a seed, and leave. Others will jump in with both feet and let everyone know that they are there. The pictures in the bird books listed on pages 62-63 will help you identify your visitors.

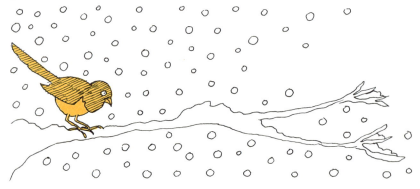

Welllll . . . would I have to feed them every day?

Yes, in winter. Once you start feeding the birds, they will come to depend on you; and if you stop suddenly, especially in bad weather, many will be unable to find food. If you go away, have someone feed the birds for you, and keep your feeders filled regularly in winter and early spring.

What about summer?

Birds can get along without your help in warm weather. That's when they repay you for helping them through the winter by eating harmful insects and weed seeds. But if you invite them to an occasional meal, you might see a visitor from as far away as South America, who has flown thousands of miles to spend the summer in your yard.

Not in my yard; I live in an apartment. I don't have any space outdoors for a bird feeder.

Not so fast. You can hang a feeder from a balcony or windowsill if your apartment isn't too high. But you don't have to make one for yourself. A feeder might make a perfect gift for your Aunt Alice, who loves birds, or your friend Bill, who has a big yard. And the members of that club or Scout troop that you joined could make feeders for some deserving group that would keep them filled— perhaps people in a nursing or retirement home. They'd enjoy watching the birds.

O.K., you've talked me into it. What do I do now?
Turn the page.

Before You Set the Table

You don't need to know very much about birds before you start feeding them. In fact, you will learn a great deal about birds by watching them *after* you feed them. But there are a few safety rules that you should know before beginning a feeder project. To protect the birds that accept your invitation to dinner:

- cover anything sharp on your feeder. This is for the safety of the person handling the feeder, as well as the birds. Cover wire ends and the cut edges of plastic and metal with tape—masking, electrical, or plastic-coated (such as Mystik cloth tape). Use medium sandpaper to smooth the rough edges of wood.

- never use thread, such as embroidery or sewing thread, anywhere on a feeder. Birds can easily become entangled in it.

- use only fresh, clean grain and seeds. A deadly fungus sometimes grows in moldy feed.

- make your feeders from containers that you are sure have never held anything poisonous. Even a tiny amount of a harmful substance can affect a bird.

- leave your feeders unpainted. They are easier for the birds to cling to and look more natural. If you feel that you really must paint one, use an exterior latex-based stain on wood. (Wipe it on with a cloth.) Brush an exterior latex paint on plastic. (Clean the brush with soap and water.)

For "Helpful Hints" about the tools and materials suggested in this book, read pages 50-52 before you start to work.

9

Ground and Table-top Feeders

These feeders are the easiest of all to make and a good way to begin feeding the birds. Just place a shallow container on the ground or on an outdoor table and fill it with food. Use wild bird seed, cracked corn, sunflower seeds, or nuts. It's not a good idea to leave bread crumbs on the ground regularly, because they will attract other animals.

Place your ground feeder far enough away from shrubs so that the birds will be safe from enemies that may be lurking there. And make sure that rain and snow can drain from all feeders or the food will become soggy. (See page 17 for tips on making drainage holes.)

Birds that prefer to eat on the ground, such as mourning doves, juncos, and white-throated sparrows, are called ground feeders. But they will also fly to a raised feeder if there is food there and they are hungry. Similarly, wrens and nuthatches that usually prefer hanging feeders might eat from your ground feeder. To survive, birds must adapt to conditions around them. Even an individual bird may behave differently from others of its species.

Mother Earth Feeder

An old piece of tree limb (or fireplace log) with a hole or depression in it makes an excellent and a natural-looking feeder.

To make the feeder:
Place the limb on the ground or prop it against a stone. Fill the depression with sunflower seeds, or use other seeds suggested in "The Menu" (pages 53-58). If you use sunflower seeds, you may be lucky enough to have the evening grosbeak stop by for a meal. He'll quickly eat all your seeds, but that is a small price to pay for a glimpse of this beautiful gold, black, and white bird.

Egg Carton Cafeteria

The bottom half of a styrofoam egg carton will hold several different kinds of food at once. Birds can select their favorites at this cafeteria.

To make the feeder:
1. Break or cut off and discard the top of a styrofoam egg carton.
2. Use a small nail, point of a compass, or embroidery needle to punch a few drainage holes in the bottom of each egg "cup."
3. Fill 2 "cups" with sand or gravel. This will not only help keep the lightweight carton from blowing away, but it will provide grit for the birds to eat. (See page 58 for other kinds of grit.)
4. If you live in a windy area, you can anchor the carton more securely by nailing it to a piece of scrap lumber (one nail is enough), or by driving a long nail through the bottom of the carton and into the ground.
5. Fill the rest of the "cups" with food—cracked corn, wild bird seed, and sunflower seeds. Check "The Menu" (pages 53-58) for more ideas.

Breakfast Tray

A tray feeder has many uses. You can fill it with seed or grain. Or you can use it to hold dishes of food, such as suet cakes, fruit, or nuts.

To make the feeder:

Any flat board may be used for the tray. If you have a 12- or 14-inch (30- or 35-cm) square of heavy plywood, use it; but a piece of scrap lumber or an old bread, pastry or cutting board works fine.

Seeds stay on the board much better if narrow strips of wood are fastened to at least two sides, and preferably four. Don't worry if the strips are uneven or not the same length or width as the board. The birds won't care as long as breakfast is served.

For the side strips, use whatever scraps are available. For example, you can use pieces of molding (perhaps from a discarded picture frame), wood from an old trellis cut to the length you need, fairly straight sticks from a tree branch, or even a few old rulers. Dowels left-over from model-making are also good strip material.

13

Fasten the side strips to the edge of the board with several nails or weatherproof glue (such as Elmer's Professional Carpenter's Glue). Place the tray on an outside table or windowsill. Or nail it to the top of a fence post or tree stump.

Suet Cakes

When you make this special winter treat for the birds, you make food and feeder at the same time. Suet cakes are excellent holiday gifts for people who feed the birds. Wrap the containers in plastic and tie them with a fancy ribbon. But be sure to keep them cold!

To make the feeder:

You will need one or two shallow containers, such as:

- foil dishes; save small frozen food containers or form a shallow dish by molding heavy-duty foil around a small box or block of wood.
- cut-down cardboard milk carton, or heavy paper or styrofoam cups cut in half.
- skin of half an orange or grapefruit.
- shallow can; the kind used for fish or cat food works well. Cover the cut edge with masking tape or cloth tape (such as Mystik cloth tape).

To make the feast:

1. Place wild bird seed, cracked corn, sunflower seeds, or a mixture of all three into your containers. (Or you can make "Bird's Delight" or "Fat Stuff" and pour into the containers. See pages 60-61 for the recipes.)

2. Melt the suet (about ½ pound [¼ kilo]), following the directions on pages 59-60.

3. After the suet has been heated the second time, let it cool until it is slightly thick. (It will cool faster if you set the pan in a little cold water.) Pour the melted suet over the seed mixtures. Smear any leftover grease on a rough tree trunk for the birds to eat. Place the suet cakes in the refrigerator to harden. This takes about ½ to 1 hour.

4. When the cakes are firm, put them on top of a fence post or, if you have made a "Breakfast Tray" feeder, serve them on it. Fill the containers again when they are empty.

15

Other Ideas

There are many other containers that will make very good ground and table-top feeders. Here are a few suggestions:

- shallow baskets; for example, a wicker bread basket or old sewing basket. Wicker items are particularly good because they let water drain away quickly.

- soft plastic bowls, such as those that hold margarine, dessert topping, and delicatessen foods.
- foil or metal cake and pie plates, old muffin tins, and other shallow baking pans.
- any shallow foil dishes from frozen foods, especially TV dinner trays. Each compartment can be filled with a different kind of food.
- wood or plastic salad bowl; good for water, too.

- plastic Frisbee, preferably green or a dark color. Most birds tend to be suspicious of bright-colored feeders and take much longer to get used to them.

- garbage can lid, hubcap, or any similar shallow container can be used for food as long as it can be punctured for drainage.

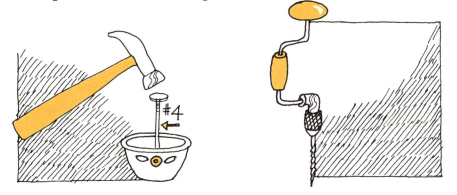

Use a hammer and nail ($^{#}4$ common is a good size) to make holes in soft plastic or lightweight metal. Containers made of rigid plastic, wood, or heavy metal should be drilled with a power or hand drill. You may have to ask an adult to assist you with this. (See pages 50-51 for more information about drilling.)

17

Hanging Feeders

Many birds—woodpeckers, nuthatches, and chickadees, for example—don't like to eat on the ground. They prefer to have their dinner table suspended from a tree or shrub. If you don't have any trees or shrubs, or if they are very small, you can hang a feeder from a lamppost, clothesline pole, or from a hook used for hanging flower pots. If you live in an apartment house and are not too high up, birds may find a feeder hung on a balcony, fire escape, or windowsill.

Although string, rope, chain, and wire can all be used to hang feeders, a stiff wire, such as a piece of wire clothes hanger, is best for those feeders that can be tipped over easily by the wind and the food spilled out. Cover any sharp wire ends with tape.

Hanging feeders are probably the most popular of all feeders—both with people *and* birds. If possible, place them where they will be protected from a cold north wind.

Quick Peck Counter

This is a feeder that small birds can have all to themselves because larger birds that often gobble up all the food will have trouble using it. Little birds, such as chickadees and titmice, can cling to the pine cones, even when they are swaying in the wind, and peck out bits of peanut butter.

You'll be surprised how long you can use this feeder. The pine cones will last for years.

You will need:

several large, rough pine cones. If you can't collect them in the woods, buy them at Christmas time when stores sell them for decorations.

string

table knife

1½ tablespoons cornmeal

2 tablespoons peanut butter

spoon

small bowl

To make the feeder:

1. Tie a piece of string, about 12 inches (30 cm) long, to each pine cone. Or tie 2 or 3 cones to one long string, 24 inches (60 cm) long.

2. Stir together the cornmeal and peanut butter until the cornmeal is blended in. (Cornmeal keeps the peanut butter from being too sticky, so the birds won't choke on it.)

3. Spread the mixture on the pine cones with the table knife. Be sure to work it back into the crevices of the cones so that it won't fall out.

4. Tie the cones to a tree, shrub, or clothesline.

5. When the birds have pecked off the peanut butter mixture, smear the cones with food again. For a change, dip the cones in melted suet that has cooled until thick (see pages 59-60 for directions).

Seed Carryout

To attract cardinals, goldfinches, and evening grosbeaks to this easy-to-make feeder, fill it with sunflower seeds.

You will need:

3-prong wire plant hanger, available wherever plant supplies are sold

clean plastic gallon milk or juice jug. (Jugs that have held bleach or household cleaner aren't safe for the birds.) Or use a shallow soft plastic dish, at least 6 inches (15 cm) in diameter, and skip steps 1-3.

1 small nail (about #4 common)
hammer
pliers
felt-tip pen, any color (or any pen that marks plastic)
masking tape
sharp-pointed scissors

To make the feeder:
1. With the felt-tip pen, draw a line around the jug, about 1½ inches (4 cm) from the bottom.
2. Puncture a hole on the line with the scissors. To do this, hold the closed scissors near the point. Press the point against the jug and twist it back and forth to pierce the plastic. With the hole as a starting point, cut along the line with the scissors. Use the bottom portion of the jug as the feeder dish.
3. If the cut edge seems sharp, cover it with masking tape.
4. Use the hammer and nail to make 4 or 5 drainage holes in the bottom of the dish.
5. With the felt-tip pen, place 3 marks, evenly spaced, around the dish, about ¾ inch (2 cm) from the edge.
6. Use the hammer and nail again to make a hole at each mark.

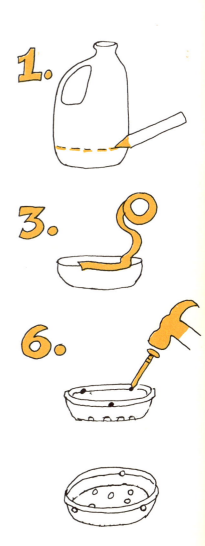

21

7. Insert one wire of the plant hanger into each hole. Bend the wire upward to hold it in place. (Use pliers if the wire is heavy.) Wrap masking tape around the sharp ends.

8. Wash the bowl to remove any ink, then fill it with sunflower seeds. (See "The Menu" on page 54 for other seed suggestions.)

the shape of a bird's beak reveals the type of food that it eats? For example, seed-eaters, such as the cardinal, have short, stout beaks that are just right for hulling seeds. The robin, on the other hand, has a narrow pointed beak that is adapted for probing in the ground in search of worms and insects.

Did you know that . . .

Covered Dish Dinner

This feeder dish has its own little "roof" to keep the food dry. If the "roof" is larger than the dish, the food will be better protected from rain or snow.

You will need:

soft plastic bowl, such as a margarine or dessert topping container

soft plastic lid, the same diameter as the bowl or larger. (A larger lid will give more protection from the weather.)

3 or 4 large, empty, sewing-thread spools—styrofoam, if possible. (Spools the same size will look better, but are not necessary.)

lightweight wire clothes hanger

thin nail, about #6 common

hammer

pliers

wire cutters

tape (such as Mystik cloth tape)

To make the feeder:

1. With the wire cutters, cut the clothes hanger close to the hook and at the center of the crosspiece. Straighten the hook half of the hanger to form a long piece of wire with a hook at one end. Use pliers if the wire is heavy. (Wrap tape around the base of the hook if there is a sharp end there.)

23

2. With the nail and hammer, punch a hole in the center of the lid. Make another hole in the bottom of the bowl, also in the center.

3. Make 3 or 4 more holes in the bottom of the bowl for drainage.

4. Thread the straight end of the wire through the hole in the lid, then through the empty spools, and finally, through the center hole in the bowl. (If the lid does not seem high enough to allow birds to fly in and out easily, add another spool.)

5. Bend the end of the wire beneath the bowl so that it can't pull out. Use pliers if the wire is heavy.

6. Fill the bowl with sunflower seeds, bread crumbs, crushed dog biscuits, or any dry bird food. Then hang the feeder by its own hook.

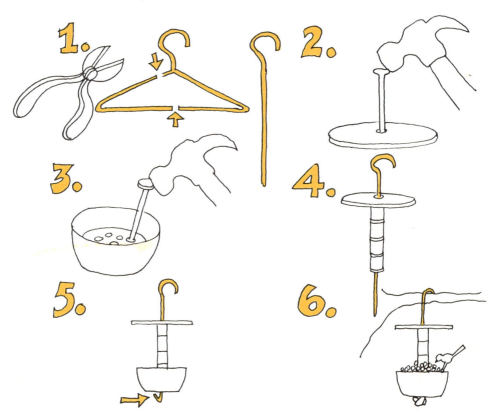

String-along Meals

A very simple way to provide a meal for the birds is to put food on a string. The birds will reward you with a circus act, swinging like acrobats as they try to eat the food.

Here are some suggestions for "String-along Meals" to get you started. You will probably want to try some ideas of your own, too. The one item that you will need for each meal is a piece of string, about 16 inches (40 cm) long.

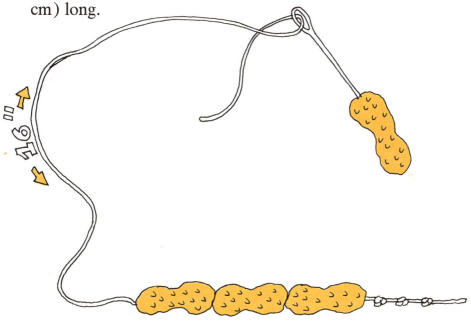

Unshelled peanuts: Thread one end of the string through a large embroidery or darning needle. Tie several knots in the opposite end. Then thread about a dozen peanuts onto the string by sticking the needle through the center of each shell.

25

Remove the needle and tie the end of the string to a tree branch, fence post, or clothesline. Or you might tie one end to a windowsill and the other end to a nearby shrub or railing. Be sure to place the string where you can watch the birds shell the peanuts.

Apple: Thread one end of the string through a large darning needle. Tie a short piece of wood (such as a twig, Popsicle stick, or dowel) to the opposite end. With a table knife, carefully cut one thin slice from the side of an apple. (Unless the skin is broken, birds cannot grasp the fruit.) Place the apple on a cutting board or other flat work surface. Push the needle through the bottom of the apple core and out the stem end. Pull the string so the bottom of the apple rests on the short piece of wood. Remove the needle and tie the string to any handy support.

Bone: Use a bone (from a roast) that still has a little meat on it, or ask a butcher for a large dog bone. (Birds like bits of raw meat, too.) Tie one end of the string around the middle of the bone. Tie the other end to a tree or lamppost, high enough so that dogs or cats can't reach it and not too close to a house. Birds will soon peck the bone clean. When they are through, give the bone to a dog to chew on.

if you place dark-colored yarn, strips of cloth, and white string in a suet bag or hanging feeder, birds will collect the material and use it in making a nest? But be sure to use short pieces (6 inches [15 cm] or less) to keep the birds from becoming entangled in it.

Did you know that . . .

Dinner at the Door

Because this feeder has a small opening and no perch, only little clinging birds, such as downy woodpeckers, chickadees, and titmice, can use it. They will be able to get their dinner at the door without being crowded out by larger birds. When the food gets low, some birds will even go inside the bowl to reach it.

27

You will need:

plastic bowl, about 6 inches (15 cm) in diameter, with a tight-fitting lid. Margarine or dessert topping containers are a good size. You can also use a square plastic freezer box (quart or pint) with the lid.

sharp-pointed scissors

felt-tip pen, any color (or any pen that can mark plastic)

ruler

lightweight wire, such as electrical "bell" wire, about 16 inches (40 cm)

thin nail (about #4 common)

masking tape

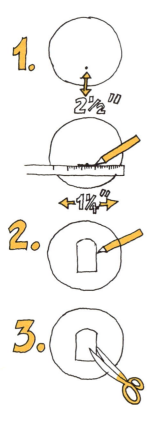

To make the feeder:

1. Remove the lid from the container. With the ruler, measure 2½ inches (6 cm) from the edge of the lid and mark this point with the felt-tip pen. Draw a line 1¼ inches (3 cm) long through the dot. The dot should be roughly in the center of the line (⅝ inches [or 1.5 cm] from each end to be exact). This line is the bottom of the door.

2. Now draw the two sides of the door, each 1¼ inches (3 cm) long. For the fourth side (the top of the door), curve the line slightly outward.

3. With the point of the scissors, puncture a hole on a line. Use the hole as a

starting point to cut along the lines and make an opening in the lid.

4. Cut a piece of masking tape 1¼ inches (3 cm) long. Place it over the bottom edge of the door. Repeat this step until there are three or four layers of tape covering the bottom edge of the opening. This gives the birds a firmer edge to grasp.

5. With the nail, poke a few drainage holes in one SIDE of the bowl.

6. Directly opposite the drainage holes, make a single hole in the center of the side of the bowl.

7. Insert the wire into the single hole and crumple the end on the inside of the bowl so that it will not pull out.

8. Replace the lid on the bowl, keeping the top of the door on the same side as the hanger. Hang the feeder by twisting the wire around a tree branch, lamp-post, or other support.

9. Fill the bowl with seeds (see "The Menu" on page 54 for suggestions) until they are level with the bottom of the door.

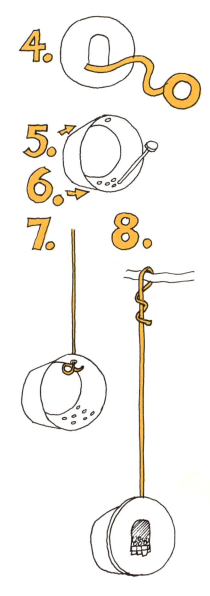

Meal in a Cap

This cold-weather feeder is mainly for suet, but kitchen fat (see page 56) can be substituted. If you make "Fat Stuff" (pages 60-61), you might save a little for "Meal in a Cap." Many birds, especially woodpeckers, love suet. They will quickly clean out the bottle caps and wait for you to fill them again.

You will need:

short log or tree branch, any thickness but not too skinny. If you can't get bark-covered wood, use a piece of 4 x 4 (10 x 10 cm) or 2 x 4 (5 x 10 cm) scrap lumber, about 12 inches (30 cm) long.

6 or 8 flat metal bottle or jar caps, not more than 2 inches (5 cm) across, such as those used for baby food, milk, or salad dressing containers. Plastic caps work also if they can be nailed without breaking.

small nails with heads (1 inch, 16 gauge or [#]8 tacks), one for each bottle cap

screweye, about 1 inch (2.5 cm) long

hammer

pliers

piece of rope, about 16 inches (40 cm) long

spoon or small spatula

suet, ½ pound (¼ kilo) or less

1 large nail ([#]8 common is a good size), if you are using smooth wood

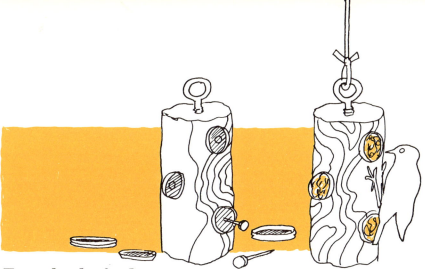

To make the feeder:

1. Twist the screweye into one end of the wood. If it becomes difficult to turn, use the pliers to twist it in place. If the wood is very hard, hammer in only the point of a nail. Remove it and start the screweye in the indentation.

2. Place the flat side of a bottle cap against the wood and hammer a nail into the center of the cap. Repeat for the remaining caps, scattering them around the wood.

3. If you are using smooth wood, scratch the wood just below each bottle cap with the point of the large nail. This roughs up the wood enough to allow the birds to cling to it while they eat.

4. Thread one end of the rope through the screweye and tie it in place.

5. Melt the suet following the directions on pages 59-60. After it has cooled the second time, stir in a handful of cracked corn, wild bird seed, or bread crumbs for variety. When the suet is very thick, but not hard, use the spoon or spatula to fill each cap level full.

6. Tie the feeder to a sturdy tree branch or whatever support that is available.

31

Coconut House Diner

Bird feeders made from coconuts take a bit of patience because the shells are quite hard. Sometimes it is difficult to pierce the shell without crushing or cracking it, but if you work carefully, you can make a feeder that the birds will enjoy for a long time. There are many feeders that can be made from coconuts, but this is one of the easiest.

You will need:

1 coconut

small screweye, about 1 inch (2.5 cm) long

twine, or lightweight wire, for hanging, 12 inches (30 cm) long or less

1 thin, sharp nail, about #4 common

1 medium-size nail, about #6 common

hammer

pliers

To make the feeder:

1. Coconuts have three round depressions (sometimes called "eyes") at one end. Use the hammer and larger nail to punch a hole in each "eye" to let the coconut milk drain out.

2. Hammer just the point of the smaller nail into the end of the coconut opposite the "eyes." Remove the nail and twist the screweye into this indentation. If it is hard to turn, use the pliers.

32

3. With the hammer and smaller nail, make a circle of holes in the side of the shell. The holes should be very close together to make a circle about 1½ inches (4 cm) in diameter. (A series of small holes is less likely to crack the shell than one large hole.)

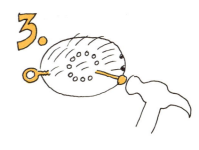

4. Lift out the round piece of shell within the circle of holes. You will see the white coconut meat beneath the shell.

5. Thread the twine through the screw-eye and hang the coconut on a tree, shrub, or pole. Birds, such as the nut-hatch, will cling to the rough shell and peck out the coconut. After they have eaten the meat from the hole, they will go inside to eat the rest of the coconut, leaving only the empty shell.

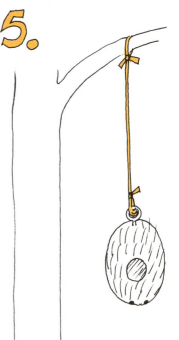

6. When the shell is empty, fill it with seeds. Or pour in "Bird's Delight" or "Fat Stuff" (recipes on pages 60-61).

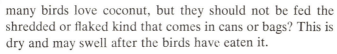

many birds love coconut, but they should not be fed the shredded or flaked kind that comes in cans or bags? This is dry and may swell after the birds have eaten it.

Did you know that . . .

Tree Trunk Feeders

Tree trunks are very handy places for suet feeders. That is why most of the feeders in this section are made to hold suet. To birds such as woodpeckers, nuthatches, creepers, and wrens, suet is the ice cream and cake of bird food. They love it! And they like clinging to tree bark while they eat it.

In cold weather you can, of course, provide birds with suet just by tying a chunk of it to a tree trunk or branch. But it is likely to be carried off by squirrels or large birds, so a feeder is better.

Feeders should be TIED to tree trunks and never nailed. Nails will injure a tree. Use strips of cloth or rope to keep your feeder in place. If you use wire, pad it first to keep it from cutting into the tree's bark. One good method is to thread the wire through a piece of old garden hose before wrapping it around a tree.

Even if you have no trees, you can still make most of the feeders in this section. Substitute tree trunks are suggested for each one. But remember that suet is greasy and is best kept away from the house. Keep that in mind when you are selecting a place, other than a tree trunk, for your feeder.

Lunch in a Bag

A bird feeder that took a year to construct would not be any more welcome on a cold day than this simple suet bag. Birds will cling to the bag and peck the suet through the holes.

You will need:

mesh bag, such as the kind used for onions, potatoes, or oranges. You might also use a nylon or plastic mesh shopping bag, mesh laundry bag, or any similar item with at least ¼-inch (6-mm) holes. (In England, people often crochet bags for suet.)

twine, about 8 feet (2.4 m) long, depending on the size of the tree trunk

scissors

chunk of suet, about ½ pound (¼ kilo)

To make the feeder:
1. Put the suet in the bag and tie the bag closed with about 1 foot (30 cm) of the twine.
2. Place the bag against the trunk of a tree. Wrap the remaining twine around the tree trunk and across the bag in several places to hold it securely in place. Or hang the bag from a tree branch or clothesline pole. To hang the bag, cut off 3 feet (90 cm) of the twine. Tie one end tightly around the top of the bag, and the other end to the branch or pole.

Dew Drop Inn (for food or water)

For this or any other feeder, never use a plastic jug that has held bleach or household cleaner. Even after washing, it is not safe and could poison the birds.

You will need:
plastic milk or juice jug, gallon or half-gallon size, with cap
piece of rope, long enough to wrap around the tree trunk or support that you will be using
sharp-pointed scissors
hammer
small nail, about #4 common
masking tape

To make the feeder:
1. Wash out the jug. Replace the cap.

2. With the scissors, puncture the side of the jug opposite the handle, about 1½ inches (4 cm) from the bottom. To do this, hold the closed scissors near the point. Press the point against the jug and twist back and forth to pierce the plastic. From this puncture, start cutting a large hole, keeping the lower edge of the hole 1½ inches (4 cm) above the bottom of the jug. The hole, which will be slightly rectangular in shape, should extend halfway around the jug and should be about two-thirds the height of the jug.

3. Use the hammer and nail to punch a few drainage holes in the bottom of the jug, if you plan to serve bird food. Of course, you won't want any holes if you use the jug for water.

4. If the cut edge of the plastic seems sharp, cover it with masking tape.

5. Thread the rope through the jug handle and around a tree or other support and tie firmly. Fill the bottom of the jug with grain, seeds, crumbs, or water.

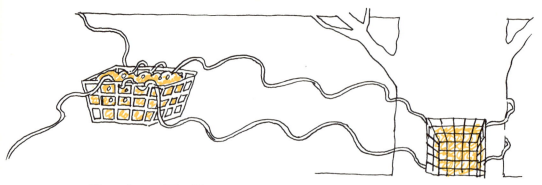

Basket Full of Suet

The best place for this feeder is on a tree trunk, but if none is available, place a piece of aluminum foil or plastic wrap over the suet and then tie the basket to a lamppost or clothesline pole.

You will need:

small plastic basket, such as a pint-size berry or tomato
  container, or any small plastic container that has holes
  ½ inch (1.2 cm) or larger
chunk of suet, about ¼ pound (⅛ kilo)
2 pieces of string, each piece long enough to double and
  tie around the support you plan to use

To make the feeder:

1. Weave a piece of string through the holes along one edge of the basket. Weave the other piece of string along the opposite edge. Pull each string until the ends are even.
2. Put the suet in the basket. Pack it in tightly.
3. Place the top of the basket against the support so that the suet rests against it. Wrap the strings around the support and tie.

Christmas Tree Hotels:
For Food and Lodging

When Christmas is over, save your tree. It makes a good shelter *and* feeder for the birds. Ask your neighbors for their discarded Christmas trees, too. A Christmas tree shelter is especially useful in new developments or large apartment complexes where trees may be scarce or very small. It will provide protection for the birds during the coldest part of the winter.

Did you know that . . .

on a cold winter night, a man found 31 wrens roosting in a little bird house that he had put up for summer visitors? Birds sometimes have trouble finding shelter in the winter.

31!

To make the shelter:

Stick the trunk of the Christmas tree into the ground or snow. Or tie it to a small tree with a piece of cloth. If you have collected several trees, lean them against a fence or tie them together with a piece of twine.

To make the feeder:

Trim your Christmas tree with one or more of these bird treats:

Suet: Melt it following the directions on pages 59-60. Add bird seed, nuts, or cracked corn to the suet, and when cool, smear it on the tree branches.

Peanut butter: Mix it with an equal amount of cornmeal and spread this mixture on the tree branches. Or add peanut butter to the melted suet before smearing it on the tree.

Stale doughnuts or very stale bread: Run string

through the holes of the doughnuts. Use the point of a compass or scissors to help push the string through the slices of bread. Tie the string to the tree. If you like, spread a bit of apple or grape jelly on some of the bread slices for a sweet surprise.

Popcorn, cranberries, raisins, unshelled peanuts: Use an embroidery or darning needle to thread these foods on a string. Drape the string around the tree and tie the ends securely to the branches.

Orange or grapefruit shells: (The shells are the empty rinds of orange or grapefruit halves.) Thread a darning needle with yarn. Stick the needle through the side of a shell, piercing it from the inside. Pierce the opposite side of the shell from the outside. This will bring the yarn under the shell to give it more support. Fill the shells with "Bird's Delight" or "Fat Stuff" (recipes on pages 60-61) and tie them to the tree by the ends of the yarn.

Summer Picnics

As soon as the days begin to lengthen into spring, many of the birds that have visited your feeders during the winter will fly north to nest and raise their young; but other winter friends will stay right where they are to nest. When the weather gets warm enough for birds to get the natural food that they prefer, they no longer need food from your feeders and should not be fed regularly. Water, of course, is different; that is always welcome.

The main reasons for feeding birds at all from late spring until fall are to keep regular visitors in the habit of coming to your feeders and to help you see new birds that stay only during the summer, or stop by briefly. To do this, provide a summer picnic from time to time. You might begin with a picnic for hummingbirds. Here's how to make a special feeder for them.

Syrup Sipper

This is a feeder especially for hummingbirds, which are among the most unusual of summer bird visitors. A hummingbird never perches to eat, as most birds do. It feeds while flying, hovering over flowers and dipping its long slender bill into each one to get nectar and insects. For this reason, hummingbird feeders must resemble a flower filled with nectar.

The best way to attract the tiny birds is to plant bright-colored flowers in your yard or in flower pots. Trumpet-shaped blossoms, such as morning glories, lilies, petunias, and scarlet sage are especially inviting. The ruby-throated hummingbird will come to anything red. (It has been known to swoop down to inspect a red hair ribbon, a red necktie, and even a red nose!) Because hummingbirds seek out flowers, they are more likely to discover your feeder if you first place it in a flower bed or among pots of flowers.

a hummingbird must eat 50 or 60 times a day because of the tremendous amount of energy it uses up in flying?

Did you know that . . .

You will need:

glass or plastic tube, about 3 inches (7.5 cm) long. Use a test tube, small wide-mouth bottle, toothbrush holder, or a little 1½- or 2-ounce jar used for specialty foods. Or ask a pharmacist to sell you a *new* pill vial. (Medicine bottles that have been used could poison the birds.)

red ribbon or red plastic-coated tape (such as Mystik cloth tape)

red or orange artificial flower, if you have one

rubber band

long stick from a tree or shrub, or a flower stake (available at plant shops). Substitute very fine picture wire, about 12 inches (30 cm) long, for the stake if you wish to hang the feeder.

To make the feeder:

1. Hold the artificial flower near the mouth of the tube and tie or tape the stem to the side. If you do not have a flower, just wrap the red ribbon or tape around the tube. It is the color that will attract the hummingbird.

2. Loop the rubber band snugly around the middle of the tube. Use two rubber bands if the tube is much over 3 inches (7.5 cm) long.

3. Attach the tube to the stake by sliding one end of the stake under the rubber band.

4. Insert the other end of the stake in a flower bed or flower pot *at an angle.* It is important that the tube be *tilted,* so that the hummingbird can approach it just as it does a flower.

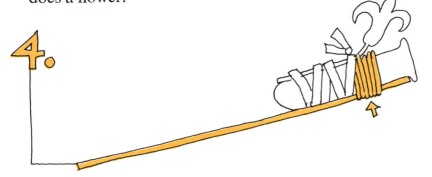

5. If you prefer to hang the feeder, do not use the stake. Instead, slip one end of the fine wire under the loops of the rubber band and twist into place. Move the rubber band up or down until the tube tilts gently when suspended. Hang it by twisting the other end of the wire around a porch railing, shrub, trellis, or other support.

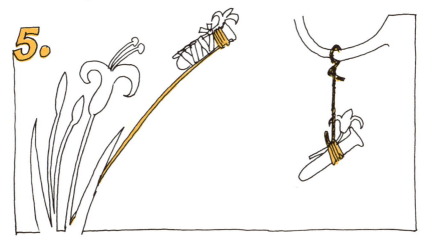

When your Syrup Sipper is in place, fill it brimming full with syrup. Be sure to clean and fill the feeder with fresh syrup *frequently*. If insects collect on it, some ornithologists (bird scientists) suggest rubbing a little salad oil on the outside of the tube and on the stake or wire to make these surfaces too slippery for the insects to cling to them.

To make the syrup:

1. Measure into a small saucepan 1 part sugar to 6 parts water. (Try ⅛ cup sugar to ¾ cup of water.) Stir.
2. Place over medium heat and boil for about 2 minutes. Cool to room temperature.
3. Fill the tube and store the unused syrup in a covered jar in the refrigerator.

More Summer Picnics

Picnics for birds might range from a snack to a salad, followed by a cool dip in water. Here are some picnic suggestions:

Baby food—When baby birds are in the nest, they seem to be bottomless pits that can't be filled up, and their parents must spend long hours searching for food for them. You can help by supplying a dish of tidbits that the parents can take to the young birds. Try canned or moist dog food, cottage cheese, chopped raisins, or very ripe fruit or berries.

Fruit salad—Many colorful birds from the tropics come north in summer. A good way to catch a glimpse of them is to tempt them to your feeder with a fruit salad. Place bits of fresh fruit (apples, bananas, pears, or half an orange) or dried fruits (raisins or currants) in a dish on a "Breakfast Tray" feeder or on an outdoor table.

Grits—During the nesting season, female birds seem to need more calcium than usual to form the shells on their eggs. To help them get extra calcium, add ground egg-shells, or crushed oyster or clam shells (available at a poultry supply store or pet shop), to sand or other grit. Place the mixture of "grits" on both ground and hanging feeders.

Did you know that . . . mourning doves swallow from 50 to 100 small pebbles a day to help grind and digest their food?

Drink and Sip

Many birds that never come to dinner will stop by in the summer for a drink of water and a bath. Robins, for example, are usually busy finding earthworms for a meal, but never too busy to drink and bathe, if you provide the water. Because water helps birds stay cool, it is especially important to them in hot weather, but they often have difficulty finding it. You can give them a drink by making a "Dew Drop Inn" (see pages 36-37). For a birdbath, you need a larger container.

Birdbaths should be shallow and have rough bottoms to give birds a secure footing. Keep them off the ground and not too far from cover. Birds cannot fly fast when they are wet and need a place of escape close by. A bird-bath in the open, but beneath tree branches, is ideal.

For a "bathtub" that your guests will enjoy all summer long, you might use:

Large clay flower pot saucer—Fill it with about ½ inch (12 mm) of water and place it on a stump, fence post, or table.

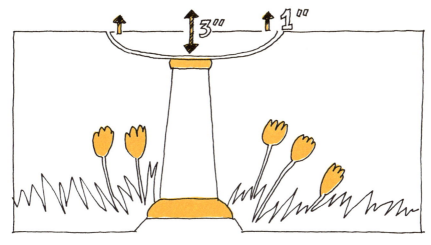

Birdbath on a pedestal—Purchase this at a garden center. Make sure that the birdbath is not more than 1 inch (2.5 cm) deep along the edge, so that little birds can use it, too. It should not be any deeper than 3 inches (7.5 cm) in the center.

Metal garbage can lid—Turn the lid upside down and place it on several stacked hollow cinder or cement blocks (the lid handle will fit in the hole of a block). Or rest the lid on a piece of drainage pipe. A layer of small stones in the bottom of the lid will keep it from being too slippery. Fill the lid with a small amount of water.

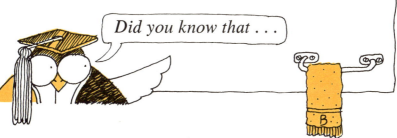

birds like all kinds of baths—water baths, dust baths, sun baths, and even an occasional snow bath? Except for dust baths, which help rid birds of parasites, there doesn't seem to be any biological reason for all this bathing.

Did you know that . . .

Helpful Hints

You don't need to buy special supplies to make the feeders in this book. Use your imagination and the materials that you have on hand. But to guide you in finding the things that you need, here's a list of tools and materials, plus a few construction tips to remember.

Tools

Power drill—To drill in rigid plastic or heavy metal, a power drill is almost a necessity. But skill is required in handling it. To be on the safe side, ask an adult to use a power drill for you.

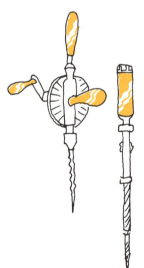

Hand drills—There are several kinds of hand drills that you can safely use to make holes in wood:

"Eggbeater" drill. This looks and operates like an eggbeater—the kind that you hold upright with a handle that turns. The part that does the drilling is the "drill bit," which comes in various sizes. Use about a 1/8-inch (3 mm) bit to make drainage holes in wood.

"Push" drill. This looks like a screwdriver. You simply push it up and down to drill a hole.

Brace and bit. Use this tool to make small and large holes in wood. The "bit" is the drill on the end. To drill, hold the brace at the top with one hand, while rotating the center grip with the other.

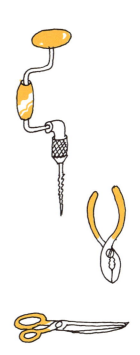

Wire cutters—Wire-cutting pliers (pliers with a cutting edge in the middle) will cut the wire used in these feeders. You might also use an all-purpose cutting tool (such as "Shear Magic") that cuts almost anything, including wire.

Pliers—Regular slip-joint pliers, or a plier wrench, is good for turning screw-eyes or bending wire.

Scissors—Use a sharp-pointed pair that fits your hand.

Materials

Nails—The "common" nails suggested in the book are ordinary nails with heads. They come in varying sizes and are available in hardware stores.

Screweye—This is a screw with a ring on top. Screweyes, which are used on many hanging feeders, are sold in hardware stores.

Wire—When *clothes-hanger wire* is suggested for a feeder, use a light-weight hanger. The wire will be easier to handle.

Tape

Masking tape is inexpensive, paperlike tape that is sold in hardware, paint, and stationery stores.

51

Electrical tape can be substituted for masking tape, but it is more expensive. It is available in hardware stores.

Cloth tape (such as Mystik cloth tape) is coated with plastic to make it more water resistant. Purchase it in hardware and variety stores.

String and twine—Use regular "post office" string and twine.

Needles—Use heavy, large-eye needles (such as "embroidery," "cotton darner," or "wool darner") that can be threaded with string or yarn. Buy these needles in sewing or craft centers.

Tips

WATCH SHARP POINTS

Whatever feeder you choose to make, these reminders will help make it a more enjoyable experience for you and those around you.

1. If possible, work in a basement, utility room, or garage, and on a workbench. Or work outside, if the weather permits.

2. Use sharp or pointed tools with care. For example, always keep the points of scissors and needles turned away from you as you work. And keep your fingers out of the way when you are using a compass point, nail, or scissors to punch holes.

3. Be sure to work at a workbench or on a piece of scrap lumber if you are driving nails or punching holes.

4. Remember that suet is greasy. Clean up any spills promptly.

The Menu

The dinner menu for birds can be as simple as stale bread crumbs or as expensive as thistle seed. Use whatever you can afford and find easily. The more kinds of food that you set out, the more likely you are to attract a variety of birds. It may take a few days for the birds to discover your feast, but be patient. Soon a curious bird will drop down for a closer look and sample the food. Then others are sure to follow.

Bird foods can be roughly divided into four main groups—grains and seeds, nuts, fats, and fruit. To help you select your menu, the most popular (and easiest to obtain) foods from each group are listed below.

Grains and Seeds

Bakery Products (Since these items are made from ground grain, they're included here.): Grain-eating birds, and some insect-eaters as well, are very fond of crumbs from stale bread, cake, cookies, crackers, and doughnuts. White bread is a special favorite with blue jays, juncos, cardinals, and others. You might use it as a first course to attract attention to your feeder, then add something more nourishing.

Cracked corn: This is one of the best all-purpose bird foods. Not only is it nutritious, but if it is cracked fine enough, it will be eaten by most of the birds that visit your feeders whether they are on the ground, table, or hanging. Ask for "fine" or "chick cracked corn" at a poultry supply store or farmers' cooperative. Some garden and hardware centers also carry corn.

Cornmeal: This is ground corn. It makes a good addition to peanut butter and suet. See recipes on pages 60-61. Buy cornmeal at a grocery store.

Sunflower seeds: These seeds are popular with a wide variety of birds. Seed-eaters, such as grosbeaks and finches, are especially fond of sunflower seeds. But woodpeckers and other insect-eaters enjoy them, too. The farm, garden, and hardware centers that sell bird food usually sell sunflower seeds.

Wild bird seed: This is a prepackaged mixture of seeds that is not as economical as buying grain and seeds separately, but it is sold in so many stores—supermarkets, hardware and garden shops—that it is easy to find. Some local ornithological and wildlife societies also sell seed. Look in the Yellow Pages of your telephone book.

Thistle seed: These tiny seeds come mainly from Africa and are expensive. As a special treat, you might add small amounts of thistle seed to other food in hanging feeders. They are sold in garden and hardware centers. Check around.

Nuts

Peanuts: Birds like peanuts in or out of the shell, but only birds with strong bills, such as blue jays and titmice, can crack the shells. If other birds are to enjoy peanuts, shell them and chop up the nuts.

Peanut butter is the bird world's favorite way of eating peanuts, but it must be used carefully. Birds have been known to choke on peanut butter. If it is mixed with corn-meal or suet, it is less sticky and there is no problem. See recipes on pages 60-61.

Other nuts: Almost any shelled nuts that you have on hand can be used in a feeder, including salted nuts. Birds need some salt and an occasional salted tidbit (but not a steady diet) will not hurt them. Many birds, including the myrtle warbler, brown thrasher, and the gray catbird, will eat shelled nuts.

Fats

Beef suet: This is a thick, white fat that helps the birds stay warm in winter and is a good substitute for the insects that they can no longer find. Place suet in special feeders, such as those described in this book, so that squirrels and other animals can't eat it.

Ask a butcher for "beef suet for the birds." Some stores give it away; other charge a small amount. Use suet only during cold weather, since it becomes greasy when it is warm. See pages 59-60 for directions for melting suet and mixing it with other food.

Kitchen fat: Any fat left over from cooking, such as bacon grease or meat drippings that are not highly seasoned, can be used in place of, or along with, suet. See pages 60-61 for recipes. Kitchen fat will not get quite as firm as suet, but the birds won't mind.

Fruit

Most of the birds that visit your feeders will be more interested in seeds and grain than fruit. But a few birds, especially summer visitors that normally won't come to a feeder, might be attracted by these:

Fresh fruit—Cut up an apple (even apple peelings or a core can be used), banana, or pear and place in a dish on a feeder. Or use half an orange to attract an oriole, or ripe berries to tempt a bluebird.

Dried fruit—Raisins, figs, currants, dates, and other

dried fruits can be substituted for fresh fruit. They are less messy to use and will not freeze as quickly in winter.

Jelly—A little fruit jelly in a dish will be welcomed in winter by fruit-eaters, such as the mockingbird and catbird.

Other Foods

Table scraps: Birds enjoy many foods left over from a meal, such as cheese (especially American cheese), cooked rice, breakfast cereal, bits of meat, and cooked spaghetti. If no one minds the unsightly appearance, set out the remains of a whole turkey and the birds will pick at it for weeks. Use table scraps only in cold weather and keep them well off the ground.

Dog food: Crumbled dog biscuits and dry dog food work well in feeders.

Grit: Birds have no teeth and many of them need grit to grind their food. But grit is often hard to find in winter, so provide a little in the form of sand, fine gravel, small pebbles, or crushed eggshells. You can also buy grit at farm stores and pet shops.

Water

Don't forget that birds need water as well as food. Some of the feeders in this book can be used for either. Always try to keep a container of water handy for thirsty birds.

most birds drink by dipping their bills in water, then tipping their heads back to let the water run down their throats? But pigeons and doves drink while their bills are covered with water.

Did you know that . . .

Recipes

How to Melt Suet

Work with a small amount of suet to begin with—no more than ½ pound (¼ kilo) and you will find that it melts quite easily. (½ pound [¼ kilo] of raw suet will yield about 1 cup of melted suet.)

1. Suet will melt faster and be less lumpy if you grind it first. A regular food grinder—the kind with a handle that you turn—works fine. Tear off pieces of cold suet and put them into the grinder. If you don't have a grinder, crumble the suet as much as you can before heating, but if it is stringy, it will have to be cut into little pieces. Ask an adult to help you.

After you have finished grinding the suet, you might grind some discarded eggshells. They will help clean out the grinder, and you can add the ground shells to the melted suet when it is ready to use.

2. Place the ground suet in the top of a double boiler or small saucepan, and heat it over hot water. Suet melts at a low temperature, so keep the stove turned down.

3. When the suet has turned into liquid (there may be bits of meat or membrane that won't melt, but leave them in the pan), use a pot holder to remove the saucepan from the hot water and place on heat-proof surface to cool. Or set the pan in a little cold water to hasten the cooling. Put a lid over the hot water to keep it warm.

4. When the suet becomes solid again, place it back over the hot water and heat until it turns into liquid. This second heating makes the suet firmer when cold.

5. Remove the suet from the heat. Let it cool until it is slightly thick before mixing it with other ingredients or pouring it into foil dishes. When it is cold, it will become solid—very much like a cake of soap.

6. Wash all of your utensils and work surfaces with warm, sudsy water to remove grease.

The next two recipes are sources of quick energy, which the birds need in winter. The ingredients can be varied, according to what you have on hand. You can always add table scraps and more or less of the items listed. But be sure to include fat—either suet or kitchen fat. That is the most important ingredient.

Check "The Menu" for other food suggestions and then work out your own recipes.

Fat Stuff

½ cup kitchen fat   1 tbs. peanut butter
½ cup cornmeal   ½ cup cracked corn
⅛ cup flour   ¼ cup sunflower seeds

1. Place the fat in the top of a double boiler or small saucepan, and melt over hot water.

2. Remove the saucepan from the heat with a pot holder, and stir in the other ingredients, one at a time.

3. Use the mixture in a feeder, or pour it into foil dishes or other containers. Place the containers in the refrigerator until the mixture is firm.

Bird's Delight

1 cup melted suet (about ½ pound [¼ kilo] raw suet)
3 tbs. cornmeal
¼ cup peanut butter
3 tbs. sugar
¼ cup cracked corn
¼ cup raisins

1. Melt the suet following the directions on pages 59-60.

2. After the suet has cooled the second time, add the other ingredients.

3. Pour into any container suggested for "Suet Cakes" (page 15), and place the mixture in the refrigerator to harden. Or use in a feeder, such as "Meal in a Cap," before it is firm.

Peanut Butter Meal

Mix together equal amounts of peanut butter and cornmeal—about 2 tablespoons of each should be enough for most feeders. The cornmeal keeps the peanut butter from being sticky and makes it safer for birds to eat.

Bird Books

All of the books listed below have very fine colored pictures that will help you to identify the birds that come to your feeders. Easy-to-read books are indicated with an asterisk. But these are only a small sample of the many books about birds. Check your local library or bookstore for others.

Birds of North America: A Guide to Field Identification, by C.S. Robbins, B. Bruun, and H.S. Zim (Golden Press, New York, 1966)

Song and Garden Birds of North America, by A. Wetmore (National Geographic Society, Washington, D.C., 1964) This book has a cover pocket that contains a small record album of bird calls.

Birds: A Guide to the Most Familiar American Birds, by H.S. Zim and I.N. Gabrielson (Golden Press, New York, 1956)

Fifty Birds of Town and City, by B. Hines and P.S. Anastasi (U.S. Dept. of the Interior, Washington, D.C., 1973)

American Birds, by R.C. Clement (Grosset & Dunlap, New York, 1973)

An Introduction to Birds, by J. Kieran (Doubleday & Company, Garden City, New York, 1965)

Birds at Home, by Marguerite Henry (Hubbard Press, Northbrook, Illinois, 1972)

For regions east of the Rocky Mountains:
A Field Guide to the Birds, by R.T. Peterson (Houghton
   Mifflin Company, Boston, 1947)

For regions west of the Great Plains:
A Field Guide to Western Birds, by R.T. Peterson
   (Houghton Mifflin Company, Boston, 1961)

For Canada:
Birds of Canada, by W.E. Godfrey (Natural Museum of
   Canada, Ottawa, 1966)

About the Author

Beverly Courtney Crook wrote *Invite a Bird to Dinner* after discovering how keen neighbor children were to imitate her family's "feeding program" and how few books were available on the subject of feeder-making. The Crook family's bird-feeding tradition was encouraged by Mrs. Crook's husband, who bands birds for the U.S. Fish and Wildlife Service. As Mrs. Crook says, "When you live in the woods and are married to a field biologist . . . it's difficult to ignore nature. So, in self-defense, I became more knowledgeable about wildlife and a whole new world unfolded."

About the Illustrator

Tom Huffman is a free-lance artist whose illustrations have appeared in numerous books for children and adults as well as in newspapers and magazines, including *Glamour, Cricket* and the New York *Times*. A native of Cincinnati, Ohio, he grew up in Lexington, Kentucky and received a bachelor's degree from the University of Kentucky. Mr. Huffman currently lives in New York City.